SAVING THE PLANET THROUGH GREEN ENERGY

# SOLAR ENERGY

## COLIN GRADY

**Enslow Publishing**
101 W. 23rd Street
Suite 240
New York, NY 10011
USA

enslow.com

Published in 2017 by Enslow Publishing, LLC.
101 W. 23rd Street, Suite 240, New York, NY 10011

**Library of Congress Cataloging-in-Publication Data**
Names: Grady, Colin, author.
Title: Solar energy / Colin Grady.
Description: New York, NY : Enslow Publishing, 2017. | Series: Saving the planet through green energy | Audience: Ages 8+. | Audience: Grades 4-6. | Includes bibliographical references and index.
Identifiers: LCCN 2016021788| ISBN 9780766082946 (library bound) | ISBN 9780766082922 (pbk.) | ISBN 9780766082939 (6-pack)
Subjects: LCSH: Solar energy—Juvenile literature. | Photovoltaic power generation—Juvenile literature. | Renewable energy sources—Juvenile literature.
Classification: LCC TJ810.3 .G72 2017 | DDC 333.792/3—dc23
LC record available at https://lccn.loc.gov/2016021788

Printed in China

**To Our Readers:** We have done our best to make sure all website addresses in this book were active and appropriate when we went to press. However, the author and the publisher have no control over and assume no liability for the material available on those websites or on any websites they may link to. Any comments or suggestions can be sent by e-mail to customerservice@enslow.com.

Portions of this book originally appeared in the book *Solar Energy: Running on Sunshine* by Amy S. Hansen.

**Photos Credits:** Cover, p. 1 foxbat/Shutterstock.com (solar panels); Mad Dog/Shutterstock.com (series logo and chapter openers); p. 7 Smileus/Shutterstock.com; p. 8 ESA and NASA; p. 10 M. Cornelius/Shutterstock.com; p. 11 pixinoo/Shutterstock.com; p. 15 Elena Elisseeva/Shutterstock.com; p. 16 FADEL SENNA/AFP/Getty Images; p. 17 NASA/Wikimedia Commons/public domain/ISS_solar_arrays.jpg; p. 18 Popartic/Shutterstock.com; p. 19 Rob Byron/Shutterstock.com; p. 22 Taylor Weidman/Bloomberg/Getty Images.

# CONTENTS

# WORDS TO KNOW

**energy**  Power to work or act.

**engineers**  Masters at planning and building engines, machines, roads, and bridges.

**generator**  A machine that makes electricity.

**gravity**  The force of attraction between matter.

**helium**  A light, colorless gas.

**microwave**  Having to do with radio waves that have short wavelengths.

**orbit**  To travel a circular path.

**photovoltaic panels** Flat objects that collect sunlight and change it into electricity.

**reaction** An action caused by something that happened.

**robots** Machines made to do jobs that people often do.

**satellites** Spacecraft that circle Earth.

**silicon** A kind of matter found in rocks and sand.

**thermal** Using heat.

**turbine** A motor that turns by a flow of water or air.

# CHAPTER 1

# ENERGY FROM THE SUN

Have you ever sat by a sunny window to get warm? Perhaps you have noticed that your wet hair dries quickly in the sun. These are examples of the sun's **energy** at work. Heat or electricity that is made by capturing the sun's energy is called solar power.

Solar power can heat swimming pools or keep greenhouses warm enough for plants to grow all year long. To change solar energy into electricity, we usually use **photovoltaic panels**. These panels can directly convert solar energy into electricity to power calculators, homes, and spaceships.

Photovoltaic panels on top of this roof make electricity for the people in the home.

## A RENEWABLE RESOURCE

Every day, Earth gets warmth and light from the sun. Solar power is a renewable energy source. This means we cannot use it up. As long as the sun shines, we can use its energy to power our world.

Convective Zone

Radiative Zone

Core

Nuclear fusion takes place in the sun's core. When hydrogen turns into helium, lots of energy is given off.

Have you ever wondered where the sun gets its energy? The sun, our nearest star, is about one million times bigger than Earth. Because the sun is so big, the **gravity** at its core, or center, is very strong. The sun is made mostly of a gas called hydrogen. In the core, gravity and heat squash hydrogen together until it turns into **helium**. This **reaction** is called nuclear fusion. When the hydrogen changes into helium, it lets out a lot of energy. The energy beams out of the sun as sunshine.

# CHAPTER 2

# PASSIVE SOLAR POWER

You may have learned that it is not safe to stay in a car with the windows closed on a hot summer day. The car gets very hot. The sun's rays come in through the car windows and get trapped inside. The trapped rays move around the car. This makes heat.

Sometimes, people capture the sun's energy on purpose. Greenhouses trap sunlight to make it warm enough for plants to grow. The energy we get by simply trapping the sun's rays is called passive solar power. Passive solar power can be used to heat water in pipes. It can also cook food in a solar oven. Some people even capture enough sunlight to heat their whole home.

A solar oven is an example of using passive solar power. The sun's heat is collected and used to cook food.

# SOLAR POWER IN HISTORY

People have always used the sun for light and heat. However, it took some imagination to keep entire cities warm with solar power. About 2,500 years ago, builders in ancient Greece thought of a way to use the sun's free energy. They built big cities with all the houses facing south, the sunniest direction. All winter, sunlight came in through the windows and warmed their houses.

A greenhouse collects the sun's energy and helps plants grow.

In the American Southwest, native peoples, such as the Hopis, Pueblos, and Navajos, had the same idea. For nine hundred years, their homes have used passive solar power to provide sunlight and heat.

# SOLAR ENERGY TIMELINE

**4.5 billion years ago** The sun forms from a cloud of hydrogen and helium.

**400 BCE**  Greeks build passive solar cities.

**1100 CE**  The Pueblos build a passive solar city called Sky City in present-day New Mexico.

**1839**  French scientist Alexandre-Edmond Becquerel discovers how to make electricity from sunlight.

**1891**  Clarence Kemp becomes the first person to sell solar water heaters.

**1954**  **Engineers** at Bell Laboratories make photovoltaic panels. NASA, America's space agency, uses the panels to power satellites.

**1979**  US president Jimmy Carter starts a national program to advance solar energy.

**2008**  Japanese scientists start testing satellites that collect solar energy in space and beam it back to Earth.

**2013**  Solar panels are installed on the White House.

**2016**  The amount of solar power installed in the United States is more than twenty-three times the amount in 2008.

# CHAPTER 3

# MAKING ELECTRICITY

Have you ever seen large panels on the roofs of homes or buildings? They are photovoltaic panels. The panels directly change sunlight into electricity that powers the buildings' lights, computers, TVs, and much more. This is called active solar power. People use these panels to make electricity. These panels are made of thin pieces of **silicon**. Electricity moves easily through silicon.

Do you have a calculator? Most calculators have small photovoltaic panels across the top. Put your calculator in the sun. When light hits the panel, the calculator quickly powers up.

# SOLAR POWER PLANTS

Solar power plants can power whole cities! Some plants have many big photovoltaic panels that make electricity. Others, called

This worker is putting new photovoltaic panels onto a roof. The solar power is used to make electricity.

This solar plant in Morocco uses mirrors to collect energy from the sun. This is one of the world's largest solar plants.

**thermal** solar plants, use mirrors to aim sunlight at pipes of water or oil. Water becomes steam as it heats up, while oil is used to make steam from water. The steam moves to a **generator**, where it turns a **turbine**. This makes electricity.

Solar panels work well during the day. At night, though, there is no sunlight with which to make electricity. Solar plants must store energy. The plants sometimes use heat to warm up melted salt. The hot liquid salt is later used to make steam.

# CHAPTER 4

# SOLAR PANELS IN ACTION

The he International Space Station is a research lab in **orbit** around Earth. It has been in use since 1988. How does it get power? If you guessed solar panels, you are right! Solar panels also power **satellites** that orbit Earth and **robots** that visit Mars.

The International Space Station (ISS) has solar panels to make electrical power. The panels on the ISS cover an area of about one football field!

Solar panels are often used to make electricity in hard-to-reach places on Earth. For example, scientists use solar panels to power up their tools in Antarctica, where there is no electricity. Some soldiers in the US Army wear soft solar panels on their uniforms. They march and charge their gear at the same time. Hikers use backpacks with solar panels to charge their phones. Solar panels are used for signs

A backpack that has a solar panel can make electricity to run a cell phone or other small device.

on highways. Solar panels allow us to take electricity almost anywhere.

# SOLAR POWER ISSUES

Solar power is a fairly clean way of making electricity. Making solar panels produces some pollution. However, once the panels are set up, they do not pollute. The sunshine on which solar panels run is free, and we will never run out of it.

Some street signs are powered by solar panels.

However, solar power is not always useful because it does not work in the dark. People in the parts of the world close to the North Pole or the South Pole live in the dark for several months every year. There, solar power will work only part of the time. Solar panels can also be expensive to make and to set up.

# CHAPTER 5

# THE FUTURE OF SOLAR POWER

The International Space Station already gets its energy from solar power. Now scientists hope that one day we will have space-based solar power on Earth. Satellites in space could collect the sun's energy. Then, **microwave** beams could send the energy down to a power plant. There, it could be changed into electricity for everyone to use.

Since these satellites would be above any clouds, they would work on rainy days. We could use satellites to make electricity from solar energy any hour of the day and any day of the year. But this idea still has many challenges. What about airplanes and birds

These 100-percent solar-powered vehicles are made in Cambodia. They can travel for 75 miles (120 kilometers) before running out of energy.

that might cross the microwave beam being sent down to the ground?

Solar power offers many ways to make clean, renewable energy in the future. Maybe someday we will all drive solar-powered cars and talk on solar-powered cell phones!

# FURTHER READING

## BOOKS

Bow, James. *Energy from the Sun: Solar Power*. New York, NY: Crabtree Publishing Co., 2016.

Centore, Michael. *Renewable Energy*. Broomall, PA: Mason Crest, 2015.

Einspruch, Andrew. *What Is Energy?* New York, NY: PowerKids Press, 2014.

Kopp, Megan. *Living in a Sustainable Way: Green Communities*. New York, NY: Crabtree Publishing Co., 2016.

Otfinoski, Steven. *Wind, Solar, and Geothermal Power: From Concept to Consumer.* New York, NY: Children's Press, 2016.

Sneideman, Joshua. *Renewable Energy: Discover the Fuel of the Future with 20 Projects*. White River Junction, VT: Nomad Press, 2016.

Spilsbury, Richard. *Energy*. Chicago, IL: Capstone Press, 2014.

## WEBSITES

**Energy Star Kids**

*energystar.gov/index.cfm?c=kids.kids_index*

Learn more facts about energy and how you can save energy and help the planet.

**NASA's Climate Kids: Energy**

*climatekids.nasa.gov/menu/energy*

Lots of fun facts and links about energy.

**US Energy Information Administration**

*eia.gov/kids*

Read about the history of energy, get facts about the types of energy, learn tips to save energy, and link to games and activities.

# INDEX